DATE DUE			

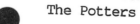

The POTTERS

COLONIAL CRAFTSMEN

The
POTTERS

WRITTEN & ILLUSTRATED BY

Leonard Everett Fisher

BENCHMARK BOOKS

MARSHALL CAVENDISH
NEW YORK

Benchmark Books
Marshall Cavendish Corporation
99 White Plains Road
Tarrytown, NY 10591-9001

Library of Congress Cataloging-in-Publication Data
Fisher, Leonard Everett.
The potters / written and illustrated by Leonard Everett Fisher.
p. cm. — (Colonial craftsmen)
Originally published: New York : Franklin Watts, 1969.
Includes index.
ISBN 0-7614-1149-6
1. Pottery craft—United States—History—18th century—Juvenile
literature. 2. Pottery industry—United States—History—
18th century—Juvenile literature. I. Title.
TP798 . F57   2001   00-045161

Printed and bound in the United States of America

1   3   5   6   4   2

Other titles in this series

A Short History

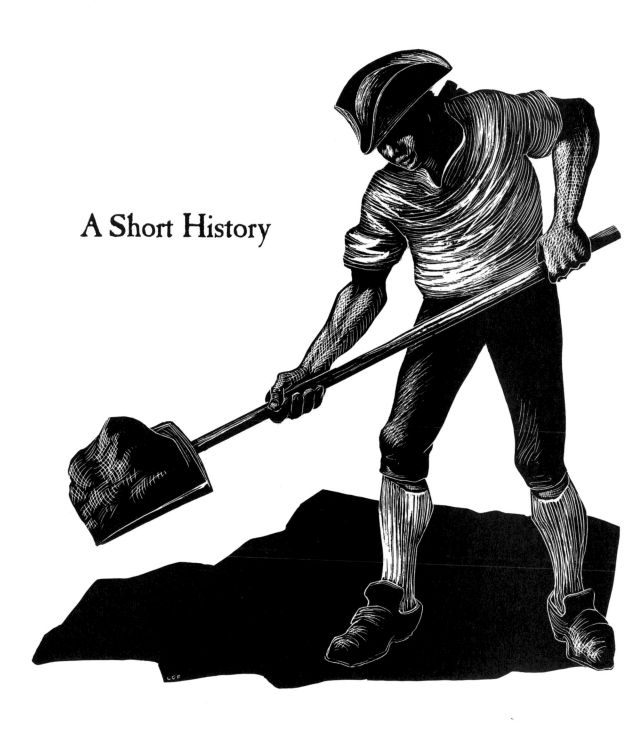

ALL POTTERY IS MADE FROM CLAY of one kind or another. Clay is very fine, smooth earth formed of tiny bits of feldspar rock. As the rock particles decayed at some time in the past, water swept over them, washed them free of acids, and carried them away. Finally they were deposited at the bottom of a lake, the ocean, or a stream bed. In places where the land has later risen above the water, clay from the deposits can be dug and used for fashioning bricks, drainpipes, tiles, pottery, and a variety of other things.

Clay is a good material for making certain objects because when it is damp it sticks together and can be easily shaped. After an object made from it has been dried out and baked in an oven, it will not turn to mud again if water is added, but will remain hard.

Simple pottery, if properly made, is fireproof and will hold liquids. It is practical, inexpensive, and easily replaced, and so is useful for people living in remote and rather primitive places, as many of the North American colonists did. The colonists used pottery utensils in the kitchen as bean pots, pie plates, cake molds, bowls, water jugs and pitchers, molasses jugs, pudding dishes, oyster pots, and storage jars. And most Colonial families used some pottery tableware as well as pewter and wooden dishes. Only the well-to-do ate from the better-quality imported English ware.

Most of the Colonial pottery was made for useful purposes, and not for decorative ones. The greater number of the pieces were plain in shape and had few ornaments. They were workaday utensils for a rugged, workaday life.

Almost every Colonial community had its potter. Sometimes he was a man who spent most of his days at other work, but took time to make the simple household utensils that the people of his neighborhood needed. There were hundreds of such potters throughout the colonies.

Pottery making is a craft nearly as old on earth as man himself. And it is a craft that appeared in the early years of North American colonization in such settlements as Jamestown and Williamsburg, in Virginia; Salem and Peabody, in Massachusetts.

From time to time, enterprising men tried to

organize small factories for the making of clay milk pans, stewpans, beer jugs, porridge bowls, and smoking pipes, among other things. In 1657, Dirk Claesen, a burgher, or freeman, of the Dutch city of New Amsterdam, now New York, set up such a shop on what used to be the corner of James and Cherry streets near the East River in lower Manhattan. The place was called Pott Baker's Corner.

In 1688, Dr. Daniel Coxe of London, England, founded a pottery near Burlington, New Jersey. Dr. Coxe was one of the proprietors of the colony of West New Jersey. He personally owned a large tract of land that was rich in clay. Dr. Coxe was chiefly interested in producing thin, white, translucent porcelains like those made by the potters in China. Sold in England, they were called *chiney ware*, or *china*. They were a great advance over the thick, opaque pottery produced in the colonies. The entire process of making porcelain was a "Chinese mystery" at the time. Any English or European potter would have done almost anything to uncover the secret.

Doctor Coxe's potters did not master the art of making porcelain. For one thing, they did not use the proper clay. They made other ware at the Burlington Pottery, however, and most of it was exported to Barbados and Jamaica in the Caribbean. For various reasons, Dr. Coxe became disappointed with his enterprise, and sold it in 1692 to the West New Jersey Society in London. The Burlington Pottery was never heard from again.

About twenty years after Dr. Coxe's time, some potters in Dresden, Germany, did discover how to make porcelain. But it took still another twenty years for an English potter working in Savannah, Georgia, to find out that a pure white clay used by the Cherokee Indians and called *unaker* was none other than the special Chinese clay *kaolin*, used in making chinaware. Andrew Duché, the Savannah potter, experimented with the clay, but he needed money to continue. He appealed for help to Governor Oglethorpe of the Georgia colony. Oglethorpe sought financial backing in England, but could find none. Porcelain making remained beyond the skills of the Colonial potters.

During the early 1700's, the activities of the clay craftsmen in New York City shifted from Pott Baker's Corner at the lower east end of the

island of Manhattan to another section of the city. This new location, called Potter's Hill or sometimes Pott-Baker's Hill, lay southeast of the present-day intersection of Broadway and Canal Street. There a freshwater pond called Collect Pond fed a lazy stream that meandered into the East River. And there, along the city's northern edge, stood the several buildings of the Remmey, Crolius, and Corselius potteries.

Not much is known about Corselius and his pottery except that he gave his two daughters in marriage to his competitors John Remmey and William Crolius and divided his business equally between his new sons-in-law. As separate enterprises on Potter's Hill, the Remmey and Crolius potteries became a center of manufacture. For the next hundred years the Remmey-Crolius families prospered and produced some of the best pottery ware in America.

While the Remmey and Crolius potters worked to improve their product in the twenty-year period between 1730 and 1750 they also began to show the people that American-made ware was good, was getting better, and was certainly cheaper than the high-quality ware that wealthy

Lower Manhattan

Broadway

Lafayette Street
Centre Street
Baxter Street
Mulberry Street

Canal Street

Walker Street

Chinatown

Duane Street

Collect Pond

Park
Row

Bowery

James Street

City
Hall

Smith
Houses

Cherry

Street

Municipal
Building

Brooklyn

Bridge

Manhattan

Bridge

North River piers

Brooklyn

Customhouse

Modern streets and sites
Remmey-Crolius Pottery
Corselius Pottery
Pott-Baker's Hill

Battery Park

Piers

East River

colonials imported from Britain for use in their homes. The demand for American-made ware began to be so great that skilled European and English craftsmen came to work in the potteries of the New World.

In the 1750's a wealthy Englishman, Joseph Palmer, and his brother-in-law, Richard Cranch, bought a large tract of land south of Boston at Braintree, Massachusetts. There they erected a glasshouse, chocolate factory, saltworks, and pottery. For this ambitious undertaking they brought to Braintree the best German craftsmen they could persuade to leave home. To make the move worthwhile to the workmen, Palmer and Cranch built a settlement to house them. The place was called Germantown. But Palmer soon felt the heavy hand of British restrictions on trade. Leaving his younger partner to run the small factories, he began to work for American independence. He served the Boston patriots as a member of the Committee of Safety, and later became a general in the Continental Army.

Many people were becoming more aware of British attempts to control trade and to tax the colonists, and these people were determined to

promote American industries and free trade. Between 1765 and 1775, potteries sprang up in many parts of the English colonies in North America. During these years, also, Moravians from Central Europe established a pottery at Winston-Salem in North Carolina, and many German potters arrived to work in Pennsylvania.

Among the excellent English potters who sought larger opportunities in America was Gousse Bonnin. In 1769, Bonnin, together with a partner, George Anthony Morris, founded the Southwark Pottery in Philadelphia. The two men put up a number of buildings in the southern part of the city. At great expense they brought skilled London craftsmen to their pottery, and they advertised for others: ". . . all workmen skilled in . . . throwing, turning, modeling, moulding, pressing, and painting . . . may depend upon encouragement . . . and such parents as are inclined to bind their children apprentices . . . must be early in their application . . . none will be received under twelve years of age, or upwards of fifteen."

Bonnin and Morris were preparing for what they were sure would be a great future in a great

country. For five years they worked toward their goal — and spent more money than they earned. Finally they went bankrupt. In 1774, the Southwark Pottery shut down forever. One year later, war exploded in the colonies.

Some of the English potters, Gousse Bonnin among them, returned to England. Most of the potters, like James Morgan of New Jersey, joined the Continental Army. There were few skilled Colonial potters left who had not joined the battle on one side or the other. Pottery was no longer imported into the colonies, and scarcely any first-rate pieces were being made there. Many potteries, like the one belonging to James Morgan, were burned to the ground by the British.

The making of good-quality pottery in America had almost come to a halt. Its manufacture in any quantity was not to begin again until the war was over and America was a new and different country.

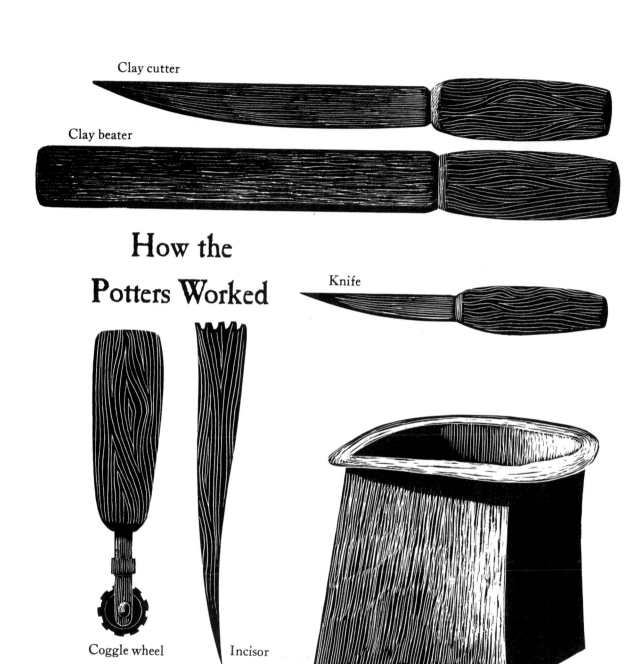

Clay cutter

Clay beater

How the Potters Worked

Knife

Coggle wheel

Incisor

Slip cup

MANY OF THE COLONIAL potters who worked alone at their craft in the tiny villages of early America dug their clay in the swamps and stream beds near their homes. Those who lived along the seashore found good clays not far from the breaking surf or the low-tide waters of the ocean.

Potters who worked in the small pottery shops in larger towns and cities either had the clay shipped to them from another area or depended on their apprentices to dig it, if it could be found nearby.

The Colonial American potters worked with many different kinds of clay, which varied in color from white to reddish, brownish, or grayish. But for almost all of the pre-Revolutionary period the clay most used was one that turned various shades of red-brown when it had been baked. It was found commonly throughout the colonies. This was the same clay from which bricks were made, and potters and brickmakers were often found in the same locality.

No matter what the color, however, all pottery

clays had to be prepared for the job ahead. First, they were dried, and broken into small pieces by grinding. Then they were washed to remove the stones, pebbles, roots, and leaves that they always contained. Once the clay had been washed, extra water could be drained away. But pure clay, when baked in an oven — as pottery was — is likely to crack and warp, and shrink too much. To help remedy these difficulties, a little clean, fine sand, called *temper*, was sometimes added to the clay while it was still quite wet. Then the clay and sand mixture was allowed to dry out until it was just damp and thick enough so that it could be molded with the hands, yet would keep the shape into which it was made.

A mixture of this kind was better for pottery making if it was aged, or *cured*. For that reason, the clay was next stored in a damp place for a period of time.

When the potter at last decided that the material had been properly seasoned, he was ready to work with it. He took the clay from its storage place and pounded it thoroughly with a special board, then cut it into wedge-shaped pieces — a process called *wedging*. Picking up the pieces, he

clapped them sharply together. By all this beat-
ing he got rid of air bubbles in the clay; if they
had been allowed to remain, they would have
ruined any pottery he might make.

His next step was to knead the clay until it was
free of small lumps. When he had finished, he had
a stiff, smooth mixture, easy to *throw*, or shape
as he wished.

To make a piece of pottery, he cut a lump of
clay about the size of the finished utensil he was
to make. He placed the lump in the center of a
potter's wheel and went to work.

A potter's wheel is a simple device that allows
the craftsman to make his ware with ease and
speed. It is a horizontal, circular worktable that
moves around a central point as a wheel does
around its axis. Two types of wheels were used
by the Colonial potters. One type was a circular
board with a peg in its underside that fitted into
a hole in a larger stationary table. The potter sat
at the table and rotated the wheel rapidly with
one hand while at the same time he worked the
clay with the other.

The other type of potter's wheel, called a *kick
wheel*, was made up of two circular wooden

boards connected by an axle that passed through a stationary stand or table. The potter sat and turned the upper circular board, his worktable, by spinning the lower board with his feet. This arrangement was a good one because it enabled the potter to control the speed of the rotating board while at the same time it left both his hands free to work the clay. Some potters rigged a treadle by which they kept the lower board whirling.

Although the rotating table upon which the potter worked was a convenient tool, the potter himself was all-important. His almost magical use of his hands could determine whether the utensil he was shaping would be a clumsy thing or one of uncommon beauty.

Because the lump of clay was spinning around a central point on the worktable, the potter, by pressing evenly with his fingers, could make objects of great symmetry. By putting his thumb in the center of the clay and using his fingers in a steady rhythm, he could quickly stretch and shape his clay into a graceful object — perhaps a pitcher. All the time he worked, he kept his table spinning at an even speed and kept his

hands wet so that the turning clay would not stick to them. If he pressed the whirling clay form with shaky hands or did not use his fingers firmly, he often ended up with a lopsided piece. A potter's hands and touch were the key to his craftsmanship.

The potter did not always use his wheel, however. If he was making a plate or a similar piece of flatware, he rolled the clay out on a board with a wooden rolling pin. Next, with a metal disk cutter not unlike a large cookie cutter he made the circular shape. Then he pressed the clay disk into a form, or mold, that gave the shape a gentle upward curve.

Once the potter had formed his piece of pottery and was satisfied with its size, shape, proportion, and thickness, he cut it from the worktable, usually by passing a tight wire under its base. Then he placed it upright on a flat *drying board* and went to work on a new lump of clay, teasing it into form with his bare hands. When this piece was finished, it too was placed on the drying board. Often the potter made many utensils of the same kind, one after another.

When the drying board was filled with newly

fashioned clay pieces, it was placed in the sun or in some out-of-the-weather place while the pottery dried out. Some potters placed their boards full of ware in a room next to their *kiln*, or pottery-baking oven. Here the pottery stood in the mild heat from the fire next door.

At this point the pottery, usually redware, was porous and would not hold liquids without their leaking through. A hard coating, or *glaze*, had to be added if the ware was to be leakproof and useful. When it was burned or baked, the glaze would turn glassy, fusing with the clay and sealing the pores in the pottery.

In the Colonial period the chief material for glazing was red lead. It was ground together with silica — a fine, hard, glassy sand — white clay, and water, to form a thin, creamy liquid. When heated at a high temperature in an oven, the mixture made a hard, transparent, glossy coating on the pottery. Not only did it make the ware leakproof, but it also enriched the reddish color and made the entire pottery piece stronger. Sometimes, though not often, potters mixed ground glass into their lead glaze to give the ware a brighter shine after baking.

Very often, a Colonial potter changed the color of the basic redware by adding a pigment to his liquid glaze. The cheapest of these pigments was a gray, metallic substance called manganese. When baked, it turned dark brown. The greater the amount of manganese used in the glaze, the darker the ware became. Sometimes the potter turned his redware absolutely black with this substance. At other times he glazed the piece first with the lead liquid, then dabbed the manganese on it here and there with his fingers to create a spotty effect. Some potters brushed the manganese glaze around the top of the piece. While the liquid was still dripping down its sides the pottery was put into the kiln. The resulting piece had a startling series of dark streaks that made an interesting decoration.

Another coloring substance was greenish. It was made either from copper particles or from greenish copper ore, called malachite, which was imported from England. The Colonial potters used green glazes a good deal less often than brown and black ones, because copper was difficult to obtain and malachite was expensive to import.

Pouring glaze

Dabbing manganese

Brushing manganese

LEF

Sometimes a piece was glazed only on the inside. To apply such a glaze to the unbaked piece, the potter poured some of the liquid lead mixture into the pottery, sloshed it around, then poured off the surplus. If he wished to apply glaze both inside and outside the piece, he dipped it into a vat of the substance. He was careful, however, not to get glaze on the bottom of the piece, since the lead substance turned to glass in the kiln and would cause the pottery to stick fast to whatever it was resting on.

At times, the potter added a little decoration by scratching designs on the pottery with a sharp pointed instrument or a little cogged wheel. And some potters decorated their wares with a thin, cream-colored solution of clay and water called *slip*. By using slip, a potter could draw birds and flowers, wavy lines, and geometric designs on his pieces. Slip was applied before the glaze was put on. Because the pottery was porous, the liquid in the slip was absorbed and so did not run.

To apply slip, the potters used a contraption made of a small clay box or cup and one or more hollow feather quills. Liquid slip from the box or cup ran out through the quills onto the pottery

Sloshing

Dipping

Coggle
wheel

Slip cup

Incisor

as the potter moved the device to form designs. The resulting piece was called *slipware*.

Slip was also used as a cement to attach to a piece a certain part, such as a handle to a pitcher. The parts were fashioned either by hand or in a mold. Sometimes the slip was coated over the inside of a bowl to give it a smooth lining.

A type of decoration called *sgraffito* also appeared from time to time. In this, the potter covered the whole surface of the pot with slip, then scratched designs so that the redware underneath showed through. The piece was then glazed.

Once the pottery had been thoroughly dried out so that it would not crack, chip, or split in intense heat, and once the glaze had been put on, the pottery was ready to be *fired*, or baked in the kiln.

More often than not, the potter himself built the kiln of clay bricks. Usually it was square in shape, curved at the top, and not very large. There was a furnace at one end and a chimney at the other. Sometimes the kiln was tall and round, with a chimney on top and several furnaces around the bottom. In either case, these

arrangements produced crackling wood fires whose flames and heat burned and baked the ware until the glaze fused with the clay, and the clay itself hardened and changed color.

When the potter was ready to fire his pottery he stacked the kiln as full of his ware as he possibly could. Often he placed the pottery in layers with tiles between them to keep the pieces from touching each other.

Next, the potter built up his fire and sealed the kiln. Controlling the fire was difficult, since a steady heat was needed, and wood is not a steadily burning fuel. The constantly changing temperatures caused portions of the ware to become damaged during firing. These pieces had to be discarded.

The potter kept his fire going from one to three days, depending on how hot a fire he had and how hard he wanted his pieces of pottery to be. Then he allowed the kiln to cool slowly in order to prevent surface cracks in the ware. This cooling-off time usually took another day or two. Finally the potter took out his cooled ware, ready for use.

One difficulty with redware glaze was the lead

Chimney

Stone cover

Chamber

Sealing brick

Brick

Firebox

Grate

Ashpit

it contained — a deadly poison in large quantities. Many potters came down with lead poisoning, while those persons who used the glazed redware for drinking vessels, food-storage containers, and eating dishes were often afflicted in the same way.

Wherever they could, people gradually switched to the use of that type of pottery called *stoneware*. Stoneware was usually gray-blue in color and was made of a clay different from that used for redware. Stoneware was fired at a much higher temperature than redware and was a less porous pottery. It was glazed with salt. While the ware was being fired, the salt was thrown into the kiln, where it became vaporized by the heat. The salt vapor combined with substances in the pottery clay to give stoneware a glaze that had a shiny, somewhat coarse appearance.

Stoneware was much stronger than redware and was perfectly safe to use. Most of the stoneware in the colonies before the Revolutionary War was imported from England. Here and there, a Colonial American potter tried his hand at making this ware, but without much success. Not until after the colonies became free did the making of stoneware become a truly successful craft in America. Eventually, it and other kinds of pottery replaced redware entirely. Today, very little of the easily broken redware of the Colonial period is left.

Unfortunately, not many people held the Colonial American potters in high esteem, because clay, the material with which they worked, was not valuable or precious, as silver was, for example. Yet, like other craftsmen of the times, American potters were highly skilled workmen who were able to fashion a useful and often beautiful ware out of a lump of clay — with their bare hands.

SOME COLONIAL AMERICAN POTTERS

Seventeenth Century
BENSING, DIRICK   New York (New York City)
CLAESEN, DIRK   New York (New Amsterdam)
CONKLIN, ANANIAS   Massachusetts (Peabody)
CREUS, WILLIAM   Pennsylvania (Philadelphia)
DRINKER, PHILIP   Massachusetts (Charlestown)
HOLMES, OBEDIAH   Massachusetts (Peabody)
JONES, MORGAN   Virginia
PRIDE, JOHN   Massachusetts (Salem)
RANDALL, EDWARD   New Jersey (Burlington)
SOUTHWICK, LAWRENCE   Massachusetts (Peabody)
TITTERY, JOSHUA   Pennsylvania (Philadelphia)
VINSON, WILLIAM   Massachusetts (Salem)
WHITE, DENNIS   Virginia

Eighteenth Century
BARTLAM, JOHN   South Carolina (Charleston)
BONNIN, GOUSSE   Pennsylvania (Philadelphia)
CLARK, PETER   Massachusetts (Braintree)
CRAVEN, PETER   North Carolina (Steeds)
CROLIUS, WILLIAM   New York (New York City)
DUCHÉ, ANDREW   Georgia (Savannah)
MORGAN, JAMES   New Jersey (South Amboy)
PIERCE, JOHN   Connecticut (Litchfield)
REMMEY, JOHN   New York (New York City)
SOUTHWICK, WILLIAM   Massachusetts (Peabody)
WILSON, JAMES   Rhode Island (Providence)

SOME COLONIAL AMERICAN POTTERIES

Seventeenth Century
BURLINGTON POTTERY   New Jersey (Burlington)
  Coxe, Dr. Daniel (owner)
Eighteenth Century
BEAN HILL POTTERY   Connecticut (Norwich)
  Leffingwell, C. (potter)
CORSELIUS POTTERY   New York (New York)
  Corselius Family (owners)
KLOSTER OF THE UNITED BRETHREN POTTERY
  Pennsylvania (Ephrata)
MORAVIAN POTTERY   North Carolina (Winston-Salem)
  Brother Aust (potter)
POT HOUSE   Maryland (St. Mary's)
  Baker, Thomas (potter)

INDEX

LEONARD EVERETT FISHER is a well-known author-artist whose books include *Alphabet Art, The Great Wall of China, The Tower of London, Marie Curie, Jason and the Golden Fleece, The Olympians, The ABC Exhibit, Sailboat Lost,* and many others.

Often honored for his contribution to children's literature, Mr. Fisher was the recipient of the 1989 Nonfiction Award presented by the *Washington Post* and the Children's Book Guild of Washington for the body of an author's work. In 1991, he received both the Catholic Library Association's Regina Medal and the University of Minnesota's Kerlan Award for the entire body of his work. Leonard Everett Fisher lives in Westport, Connecticut.